Blue Morning Glory
(chart on pg. 2)

X	DMC	¼X	B'ST	ANC.	COLOR
═	153				lt blue
∞	159				blue
X	160				dk blue
▪▪	161				vy dk blue
◥	300			352	rust
▼	310	◢	╱	403	black
T	311			148	lt navy blue
▬	433			358	tan
★	434	◢	╱	310	lt tan
θ	676			891	lt gold
△	677			886	vy lt gold
∷	680		╱	901	dk gold
⊬	729			890	gold
╲	746		╱	275	yellow
✛	772			259	vy lt green
M	780			309	topaz
6	781			308	lt topaz
◆	801		╱	359	brown
Σ	823			152	navy blue
◀	3345		╱	268	vy dk green
⊞	3346			267	dk green
⋈	3347			266	green
3	3348	◩		264	lt green
╲	3747			120	vy lt blue
H	3834			100	violet
✳	3835			98	lt violet
4	3836			90	vy lt violet
●	433			358	tan Fr. Knot

The design was stitched on a 12" x 14" piece of 28 count Cream Cashel Linen® over two fabric threads (design size 5⅞" x 8"). Two strands of floss were used for Cross Stitch and 1 strand for Backstitch and French Knots. It was custom framed.

Stitch Count (82w x 111h)
14 count	5⅞"	x	8"
16 count	5⅛"	x	7"
18 count	4⅝"	x	6¼"

Trumpetvine (chart on pg. 3)

X	DMC	¼X	B'ST	ANC.	COLOR
∞	159				blue
▼	310	◢	╱	403	black
P	350			11	dk coral
L	351			10	coral
⊠	352		╱	9	lt coral
	356		╱	5975	lt rust
←	402			1047	lt copper
♠	433		╱	358	dk tan
◆	434		◢	310	tan
▢	436			1045	lt tan
∷	680			901	vy dk gold
✛	772			259	vy lt green
⊬	729			890	gold
╲	746		╱	275	yellow
⊮	777				maroon
6	801			359	brown
G	921			1003	dk copper
◀	3345		╱	268	vy dk green
⊞	3346			267	dk green
⋈	3347			266	green
3	3348	◩		264	lt green
H	3350		╱	59	dk pink
✳	3731			76	pink
4	3733			75	lt pink
И	3776			1048	copper
	3777		╱	1015	rust
8	3831			29	rose
♡	3832			28	lt rose
⁄⁄	3856			1010	vy lt copper
●	352			9	lt coral Fr. Knot

The design was stitched on a 12" x 14" piece of 28 count Cream Cashel Linen® over two fabric threads (design size 5⅞" x 7⅞"). Two strands of floss were used for Cross Stitch and 1 strand for Backstitch and French Knots. It was custom framed.

Stitch Count (82w x 109h)
14 count	5⅞"	x	7⅞"
16 count	5⅛"	x	6⅞"
18 count	4⅝"	x	6⅛"

Needlework adaptation by Carol Emmer.

We have made every effort to ensure that these instructions are accurate and complete. We cannot, however, be responsible for human error, typographical mistakes, or variations in individual work.

Fabric provided courtesy of Zweigart®.

Embroidery floss provided courtesy of The DMC Corporation.

Production Team: Writer – Carolyn Breeding; Graphic Artist – John Rose; and Photo Stylist – Christy Myers.

Instructions tested and some photo models made by Muriel Hicks.

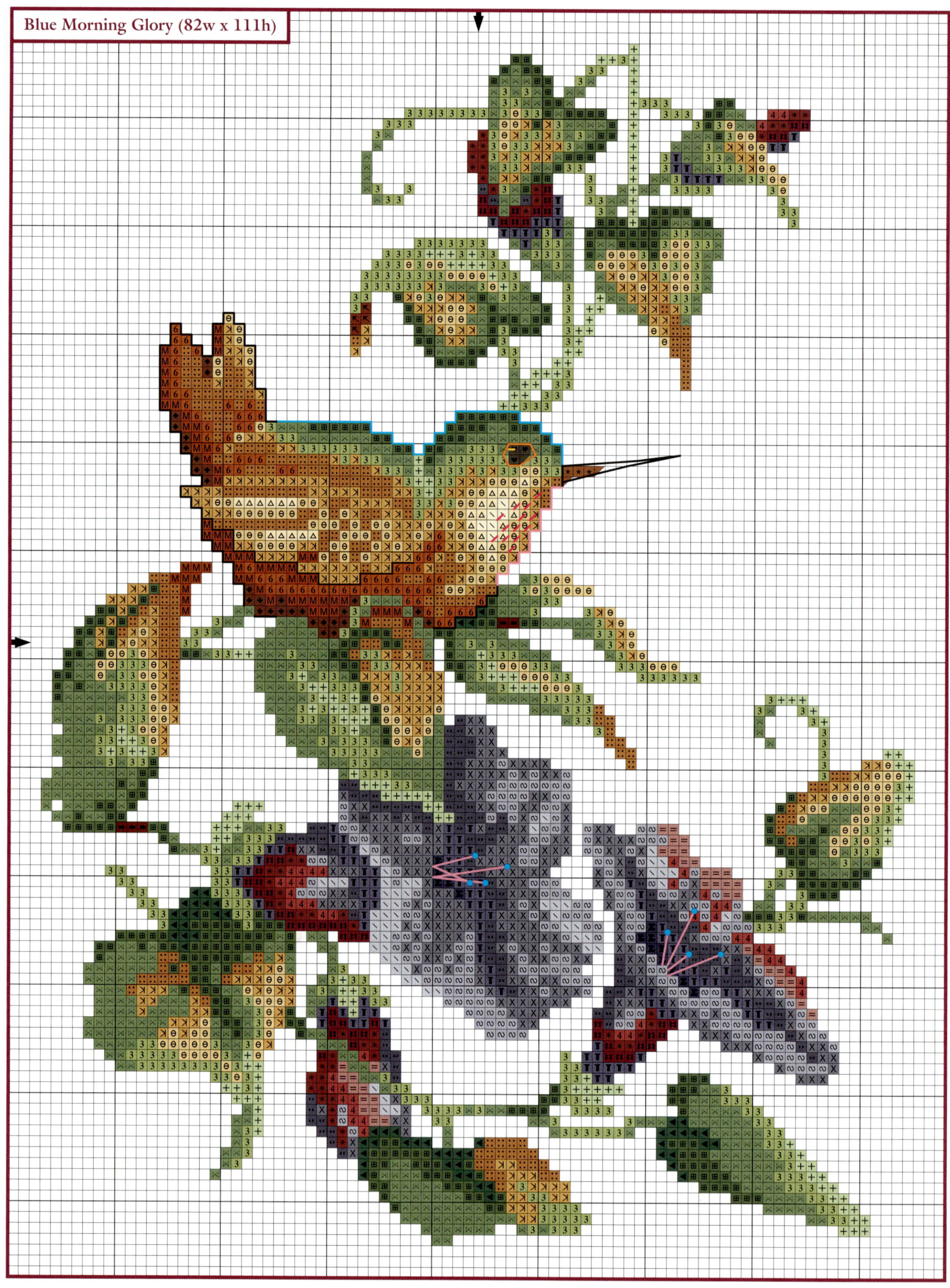

Blue Morning Glory (82w x 111h)

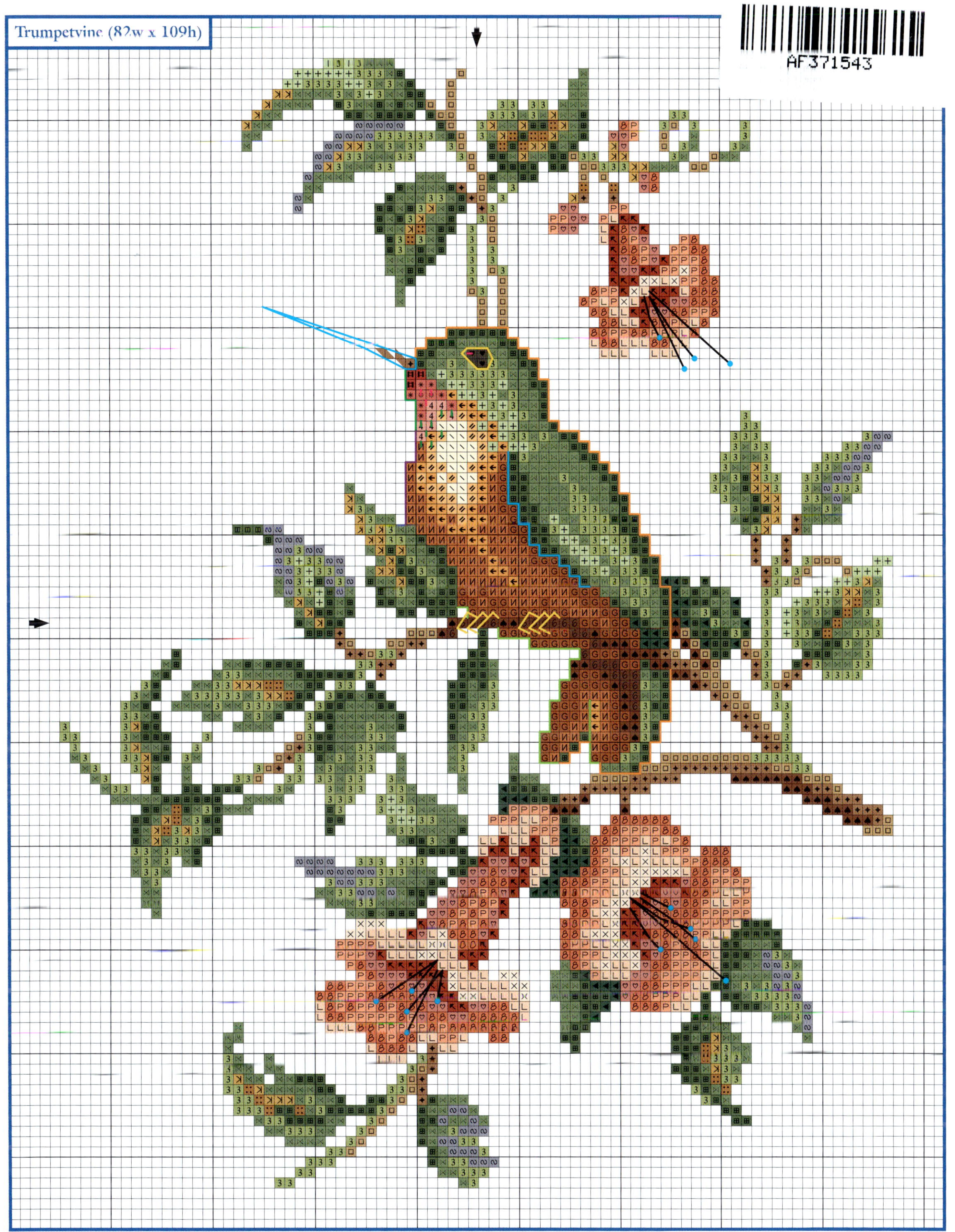

Garden Tulips

X	DMC	¼X	½X	B'ST	ANC.	COLOR		X	DMC	¼X	B'ST	ANC.	COLOR
	310	◢		╱	403	black			729	◺		890	gold
	333				119	vy dk purple			746		╱	275	vy lt yellow
	340				118	purple			772			259	vy lt green
	341				117	lt purple			777				dk garnet
	433	◢		╱	358	dk brown			780		╱	309	dk topaz
	436		♠		1045	brown			781			308	topaz
	437		♣		362	lt brown			782			307	lt topaz
	676				891	lt gold			791			178	lt blue
	677				886	vy lt gold			814			45	vy dk garnet
	680			╱	901	dk gold			823			152	blue
	725				305	yellow			934			862	forest green
	726				295	lt yellow			3345		╱	268	vy dk green
	728					dk yellow			3346			267	dk green

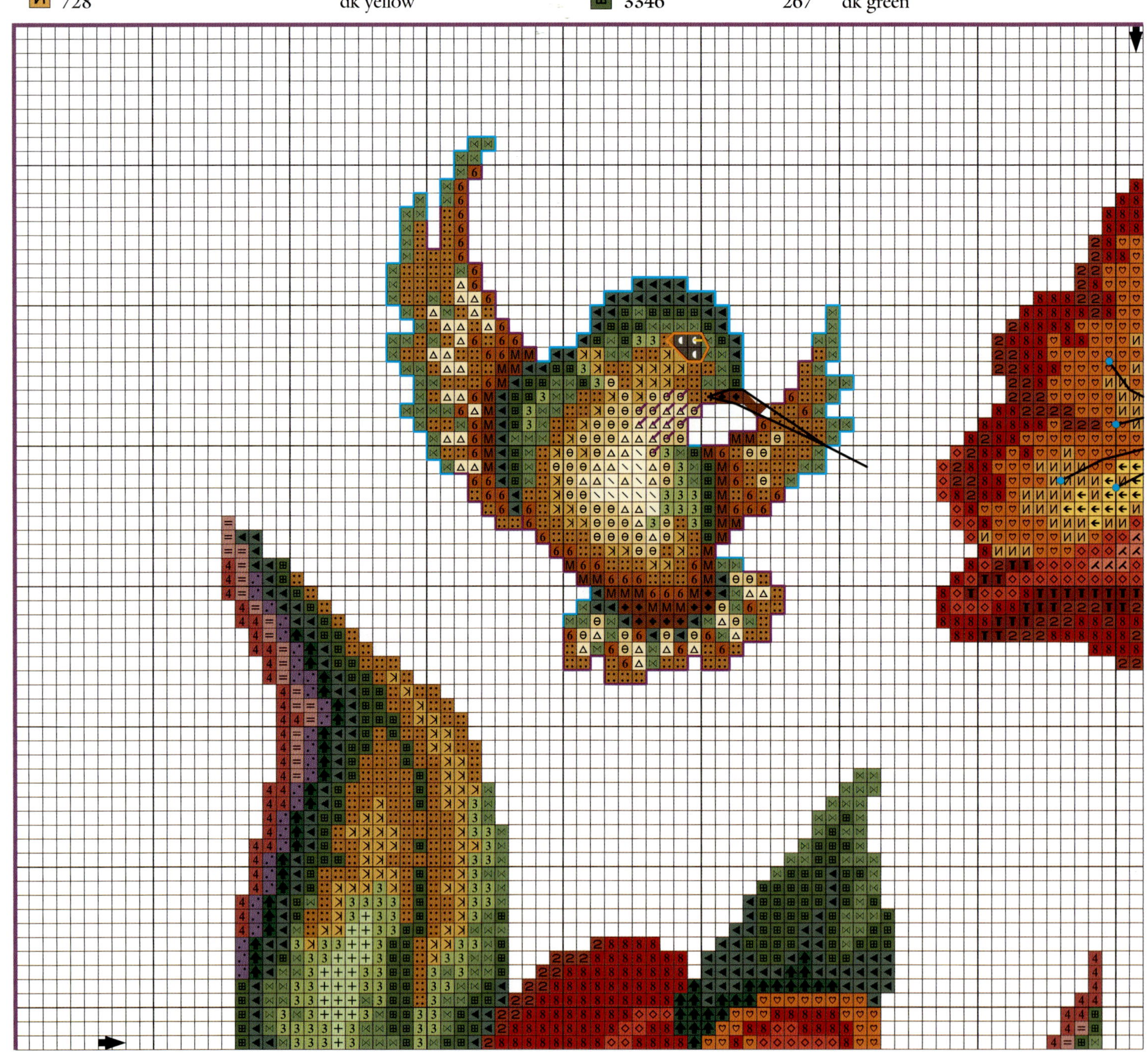

X	DMC	ANC.	COLOR
⊠	3347	266	green
3	3348	264	lt green
∴	3746	1030	dk purple
✖	3747	120	vy lt purple
8	3831	29	garnet
◇	3832	28	lt garnet
✂	3833	26	vy lt garnet
4	3835	98	violet
=	3836	90	lt violet
●	433	358	dk brown Fr. Knot

Grey area indicates last row of previous section of design.

The design was stitched on a 16" x 16" piece of 28 count Cream Cashel Linen® over two fabric threads (design size 9⅞" x 10"). Two strands of floss were used for Cross Stitch and 1 strand for Half Cross Stitch, Backstitch, and French Knots. It was custom framed.

Stitch Count (145w x 139h)

count	width		height
14 count	9⅞"	x	10"
16 count	8⅝"	x	8¾"
18 count	7⅝"	x	7¾"

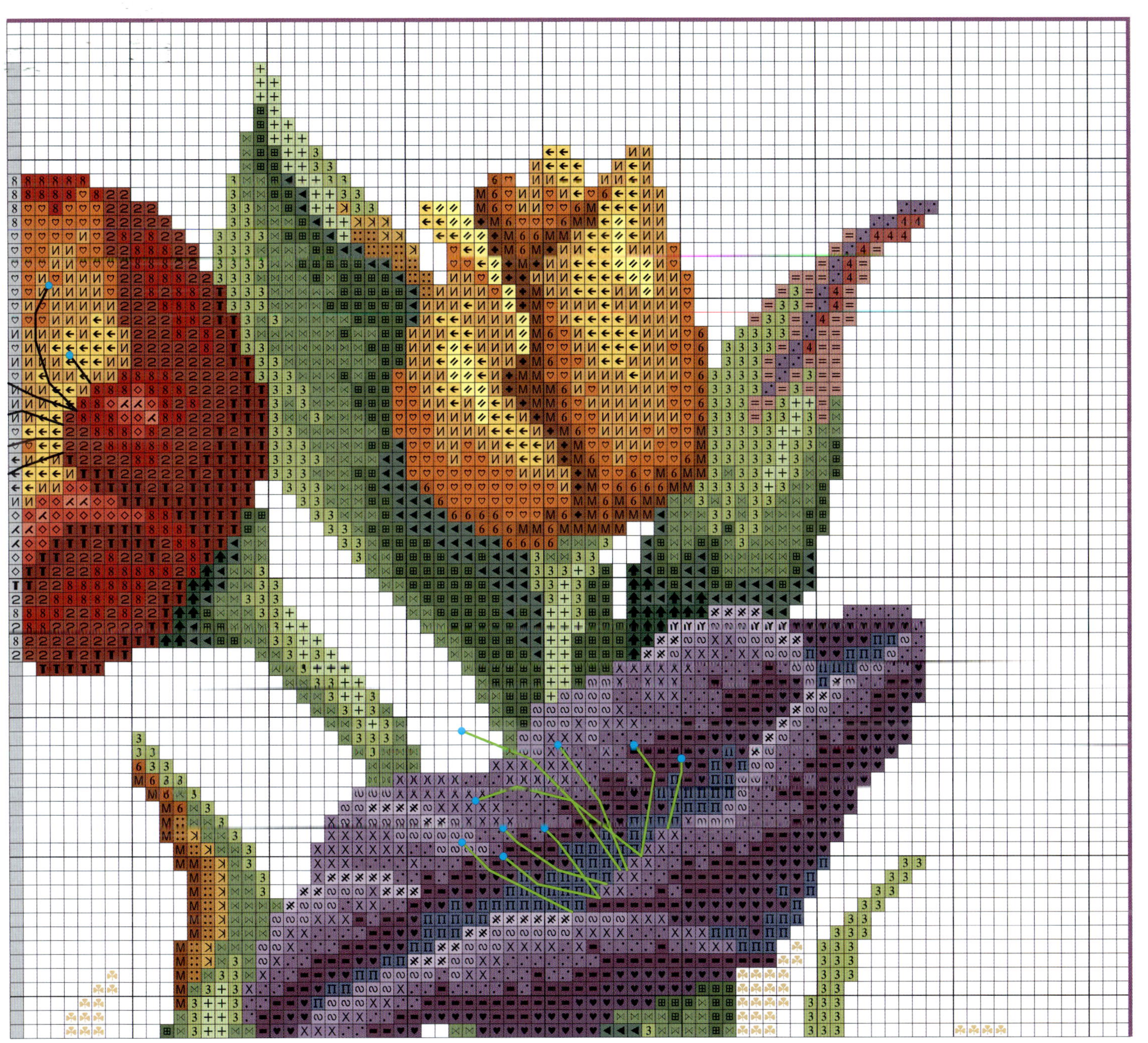

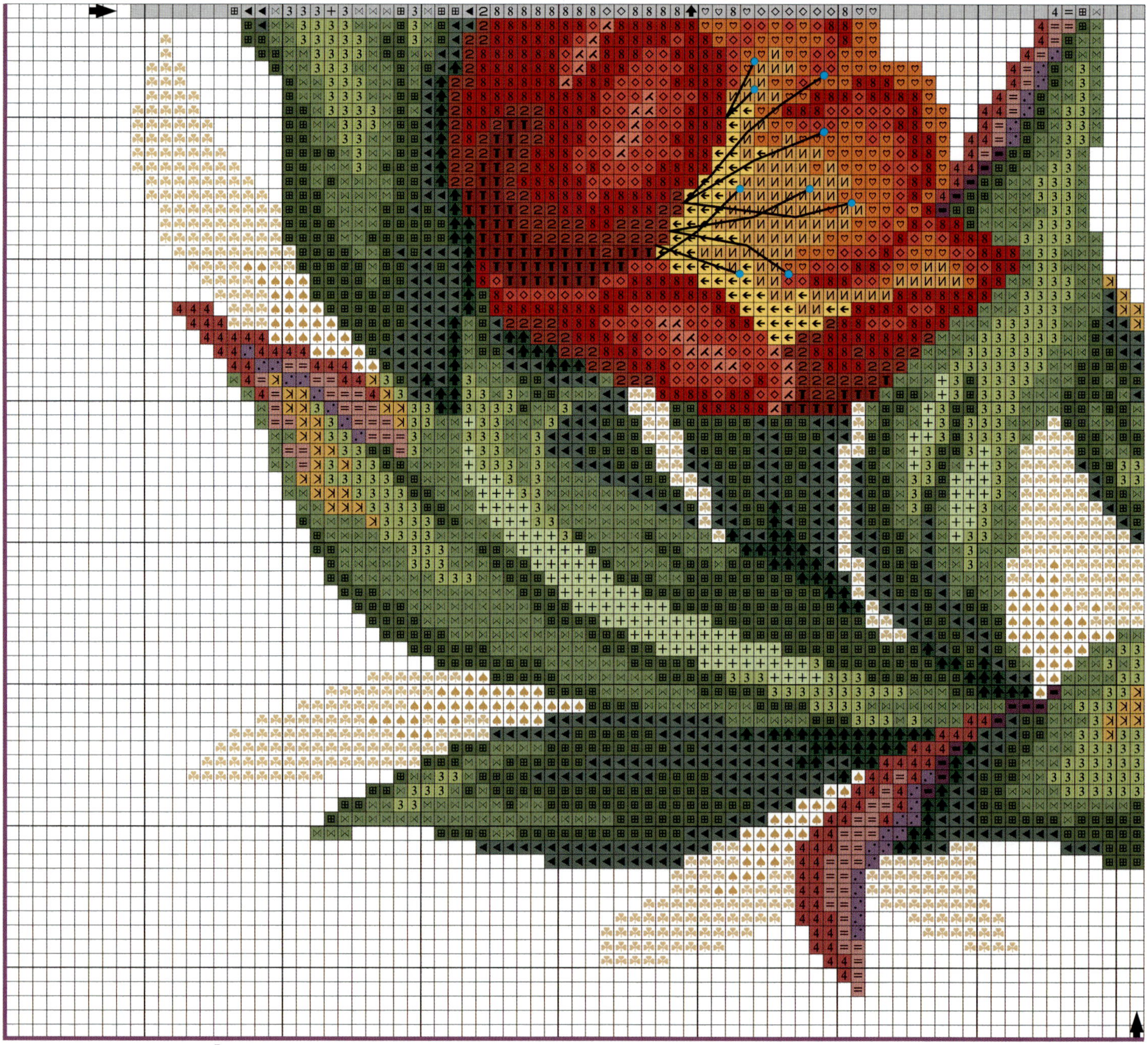

Garden Tulips

X	DMC	1/4X	1/2X	B'ST	ANC.	COLOR
	310	◪		/	403	black
	333				119	vy dk purple
	340				118	purple
	341				117	lt purple
	433	◪		/	358	dk brown
	436		♠		1045	brown
	437		☘		362	lt brown
	676				891	lt gold
	677				886	vy lt gold
	680			/	901	dk gold
	725				305	yellow
	726				295	lt yellow
	728					dk yellow

X	DMC	1/4X	B'ST	ANC.	COLOR
	729	◪		890	gold
	746		/	275	vy lt yellow
	772			259	vy lt green
	777				dk garnet
	780		/	309	dk topaz
	781			308	topaz
	782			307	lt topaz
	791			178	lt blue
	814			45	vy dk garnet
	823			152	blue
	934			862	forest green
	3345		/	268	vy dk green
	3346			267	dk green

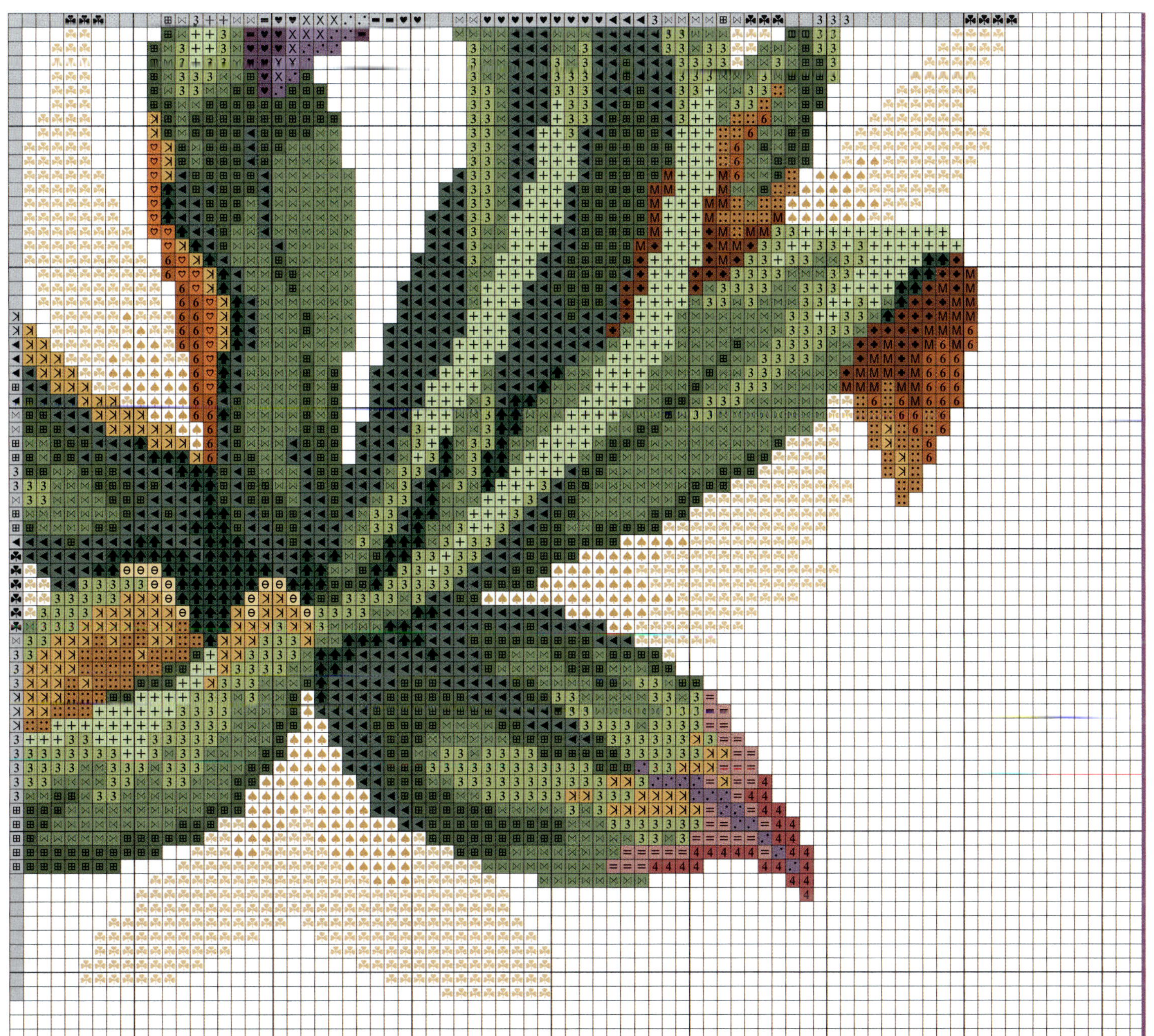

X	DMC	ANC.	COLOR
⊠	3347	266	green
3	3348	264	lt green
⬟	3746	1030	dk purple
✷	3747	120	vy lt purple
8	3831	29	garnet
◇	3832	28	lt garnet
⤡	3833	26	vy lt garnet
4	3835	98	violet
═	3836	90	lt violet
●	433	358	dk brown Fr. Knot
	Grey area indicates last row of previous section of design.		

Garden Lilies

X	DMC	¼X	½X	B'ST	ANC.	COLOR		X	DMC	¼X	B'ST	ANC.	COLOR
◖	310	◣		╱	403	black		⁄	726			295	lt yellow
■	333				119	vy dk purple		И	728				dk yellow
X	340				118	purple		K	729			890	gold
∽	341				117	lt purple		＼	746		╱	275	vy lt yellow
◨	350				11	dk coral		+	772			259	vy lt green
∧	351				10	coral		✳	777		◣		garnet
⊥	352				9	lt coral		M	780		╱	309	dk topaz
✦	433	�		╱	358	lt brown		6	781			308	topaz
	436		♠		1045	tan		♡	782			307	lt topaz
	437		Σ		362	lt tan		♥	791			178	lt blue
Θ	676				891	lt gold		Ｔ	814		╱	45	dk garnet
△	677				886	vy lt gold		Π	823			152	blue
⠿	680			╱	901	dk gold		Σ	934			862	avocado
←	725				305	yellow		✕	938			381	brown

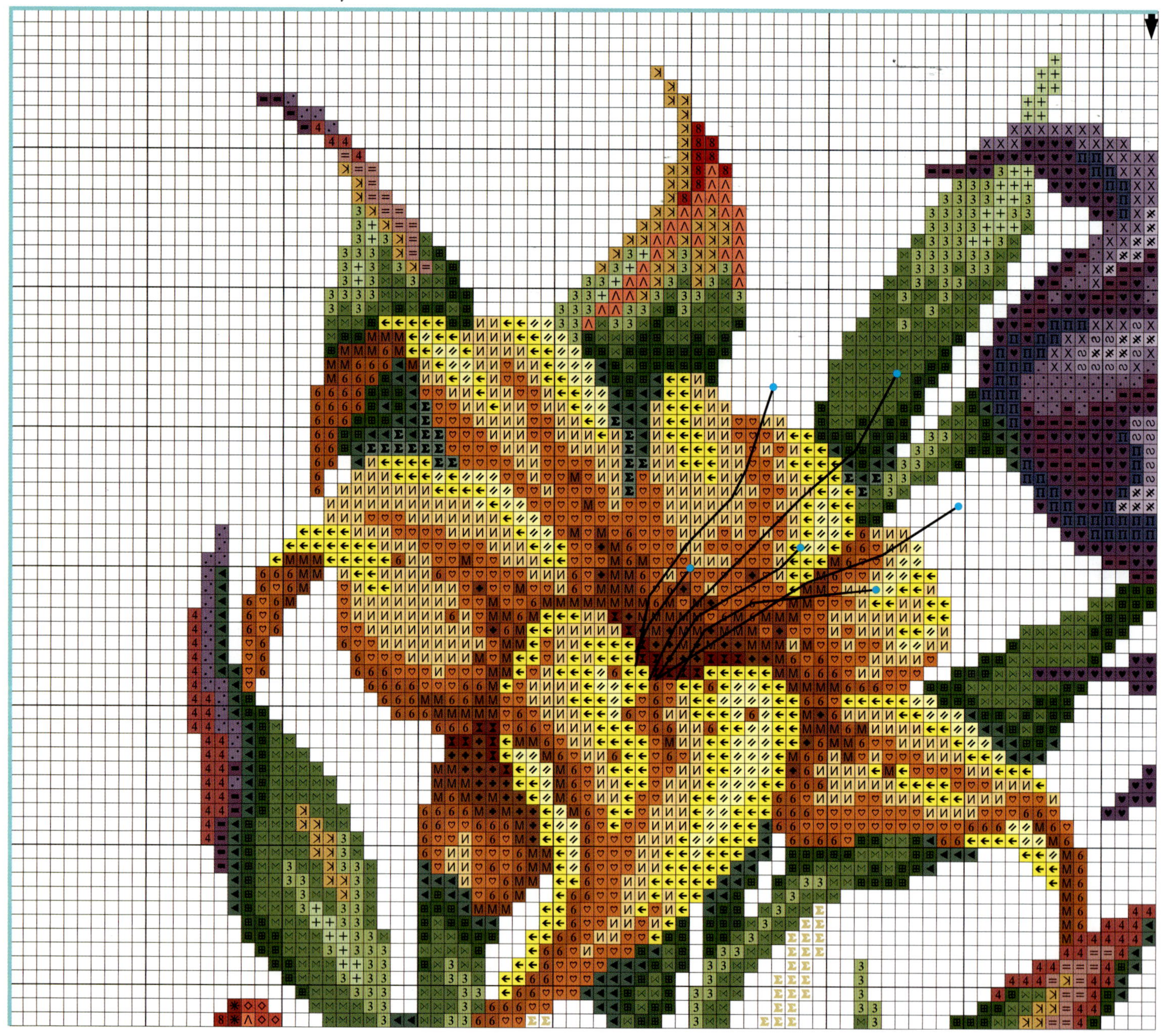

X	DMC	¼X	B'ST	ANC.	COLOR
◄	3345		╱	268	vy dk green
⊞	3346			267	dk green
⊠	3347	◩	◩	266	green
3	3348			264	lt green
⬩	3746			1030	dk purple
✳	3747			120	vy lt purple
8	3831			29	lt garnet
◇	3832			28	vy lt garnet
4	3835			98	violet
=	3836			90	lt violet
•	433			358	lt brown Fr. Knot
▨					Grey area indicates last row of previous section of design.

The design was stitched on a 16½" x 16" piece of 28 count Cream Cashel Linen® over two fabric threads (design size 10¼" x 10"). Two strands of floss were used for Cross Stitch and 1 strand for Half Cross Stitch, Backstitch, and French Knots. It was custom framed.

Stitch Count (143w x 139h)

14 count	10¼"	x	10"
16 count	9"	x	8¾"
18 count	8"	x	7¾"

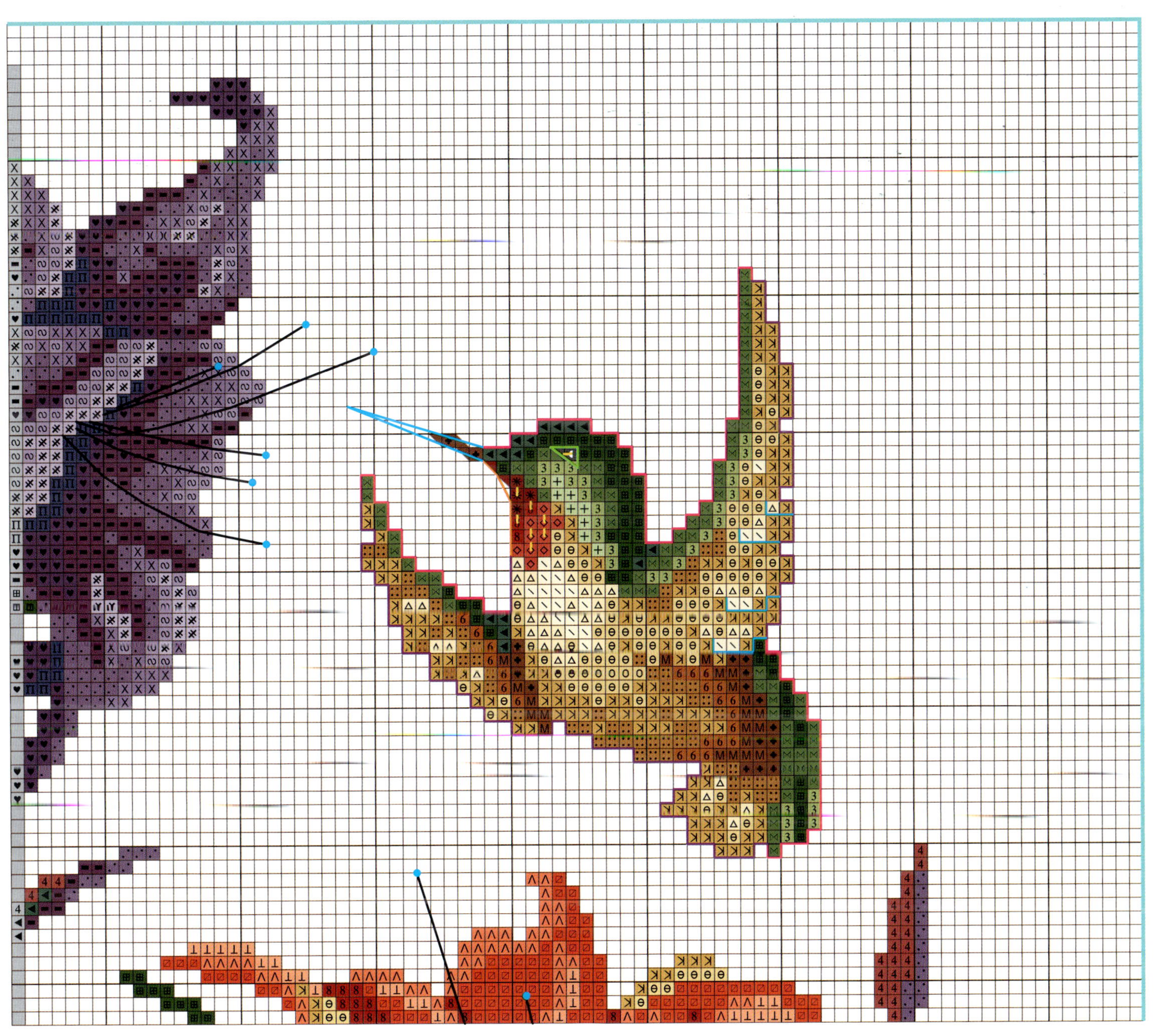

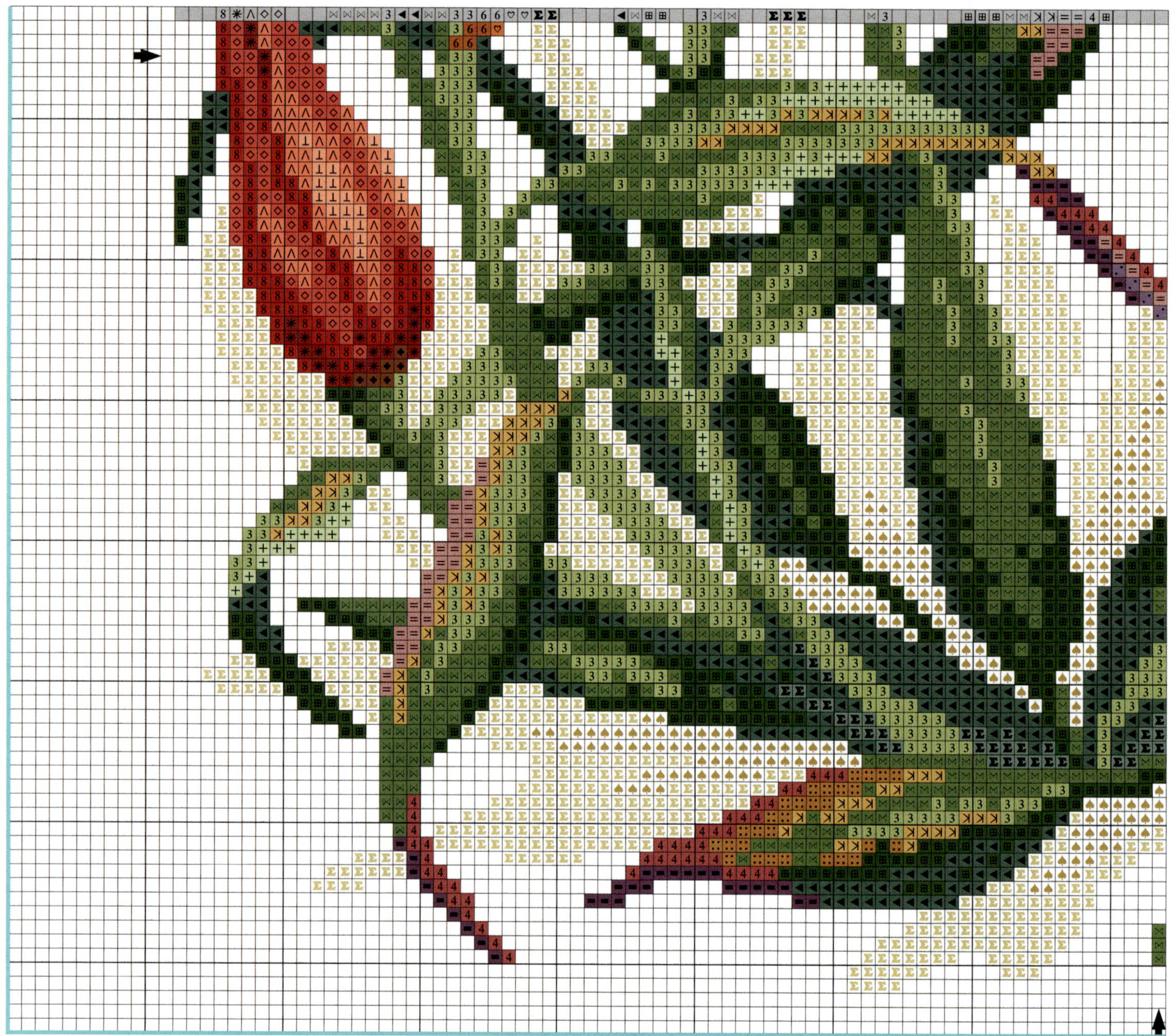

Garden Lilies

X	DMC	1/4X	1/2X	B'ST	ANC.	COLOR
	310	◢		╱	403	black
	333				119	vy dk purple
	340				118	purple
	341				117	lt purple
	350				11	dk coral
	351				10	coral
	352				9	lt coral
	433	◢		╱	358	lt brown
	436		♠		1045	tan
	437		Σ		362	lt tan
	676				891	lt gold
	677				886	vy lt gold
	680			╱	901	dk gold
	725				305	yellow

X	DMC	1/4X	B'ST	ANC.	COLOR
	726			295	lt yellow
	728				dk yellow
	729			890	gold
	746		╱	275	vy lt yellow
	772			259	vy lt green
	777	◢			garnet
	780		╱	309	dk topaz
	781			308	topaz
	782			307	lt topaz
	791			178	lt blue
	814		╱	45	dk garnet
	823			152	blue
	934			862	avocado
	938			381	brown

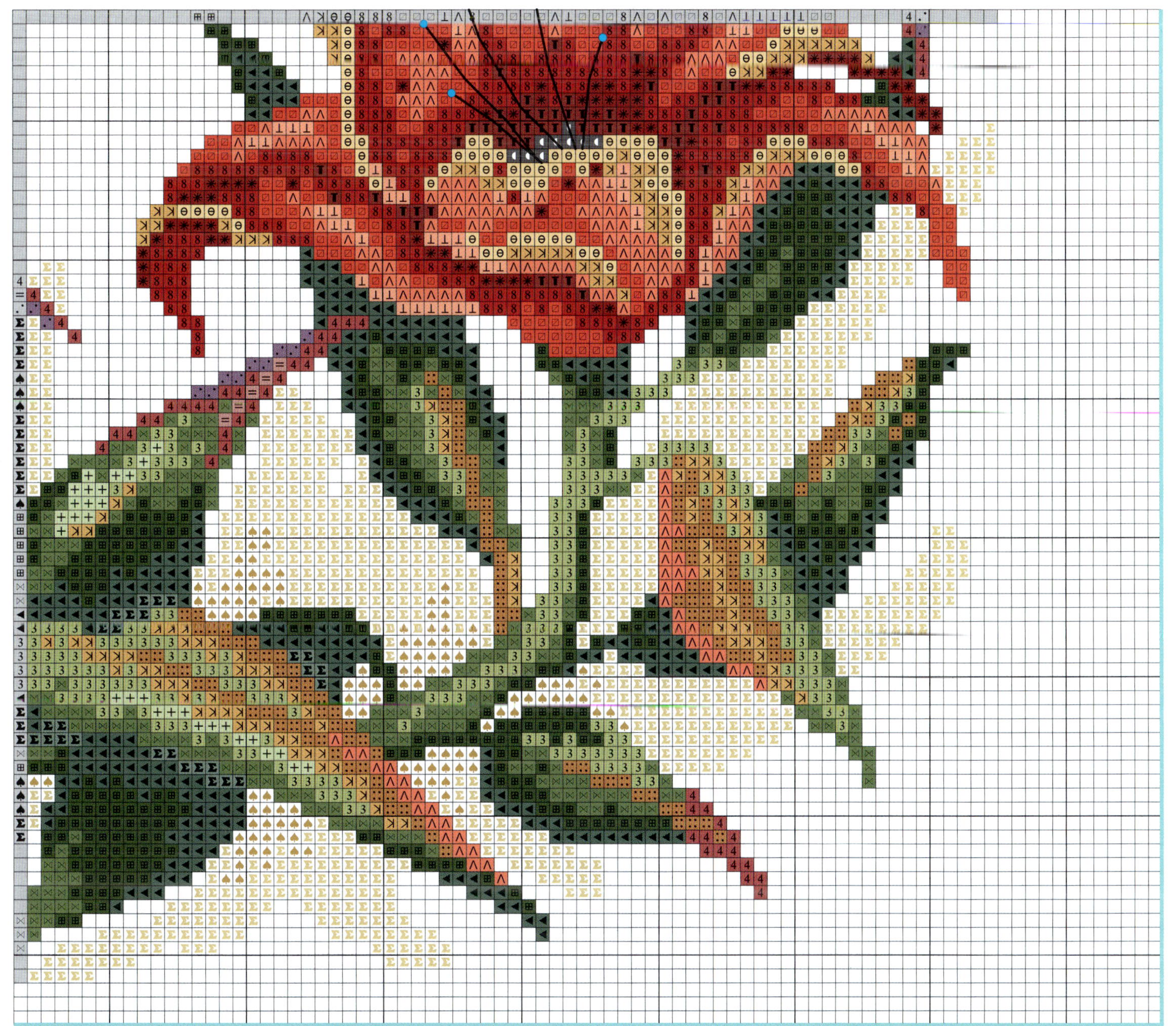

X	DMC	¼X	B'ST	ANC.	COLOR
◀	3345		╱	268	vy dk green
⊞	3346			267	dk green
⋈	3347	◣		266	green
3	3348			264	lt green
	3716			1030	dk purple
✶	3747			120	vy lt purple
8	3831			29	lt garnet
◇	3832			28	vy lt garnet
4	3835			98	violet
=	3836			90	lt violet
●	433			358	lt brown Fr. Knot
	Grey area indicates last row of previous section of design.				

How to Read Charts

Each chart is made up of a key and a gridded design where each square represents a stitch. The symbols in the key tell which floss color to use for each stitch in the chart. The following headings and symbols are given:

X — Cross Stitch
DMC — DMC color number
1/4 X — Quarter Stitch
1/2 X — Half Cross Stitch
B'ST — Backstitch
ANC. — Anchor color number
COLOR — the name given to the floss color in this chart

A square filled with a color and a symbol should be worked as a **Cross Stitch**.

A triangle should be worked as a **Quarter Stitch**.

A square containing a colored symbol should be worked as a **Half Cross Stitch**.

A straight line should be worked as a **Backstitch**.

A large dot listed near the end of the key should be worked as a **French Knot**.

Sometimes the symbol for a Cross Stitch may be partially covered when a Backstitch crosses the square. Refer to the background color to determine the floss color.

How to Stitch

Always work **Cross Stitches**, **Quarter Stitches**, and **Half Cross Stitches** first and then add the **Backstitch** and **French Knots**.

Cross Stitch (X): For horizontal rows, work stitches in two journeys *(Fig. 1)*. For vertical rows, complete each stitch as shown *(Fig. 2)*. When working over two fabric threads, work Cross Stitch as shown in **Fig. 3**.

Fig. 1

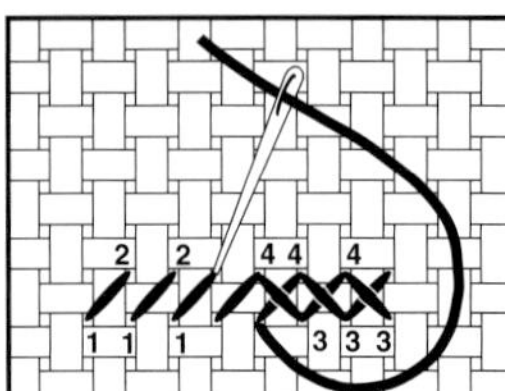

Fig. 2

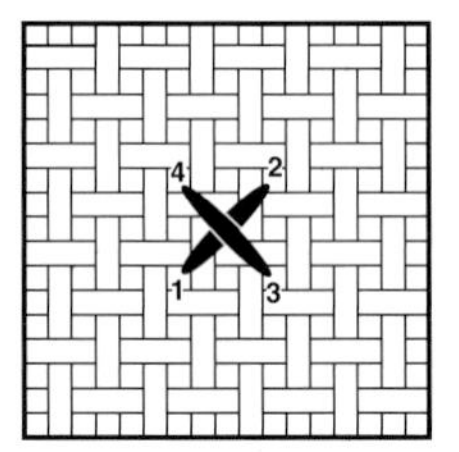

Fig. 3

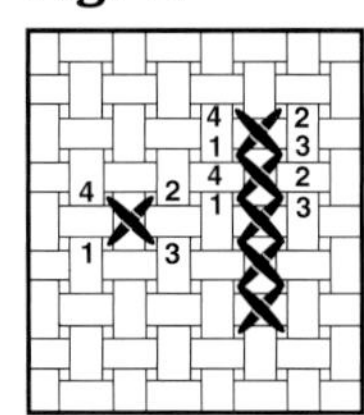

Quarter Stitch (1/4X): Come up at 1 *(Fig. 4)*, then split fabric thread to go down at 2. **Fig. 5** shows the technique for Quarter Stitch when working over two fabric threads.

Fig. 4

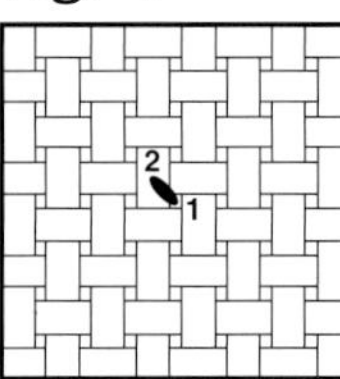

Fig. 5

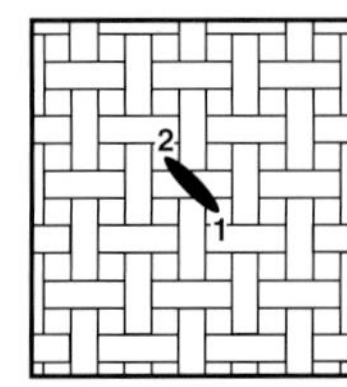

Half Cross Stitch (1/2X): This stitch is one journey of the Cross Stitch and is worked from lower left to upper right as shown in **Fig. 6**. When working over two fabric threads, work Half Cross Stitch as shown in **Fig. 7**.

Fig. 6

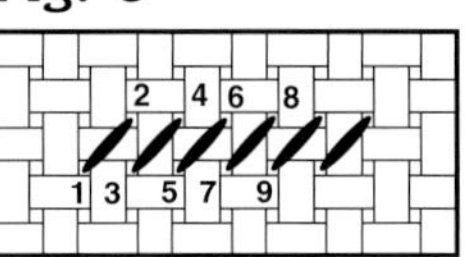

Fig. 7

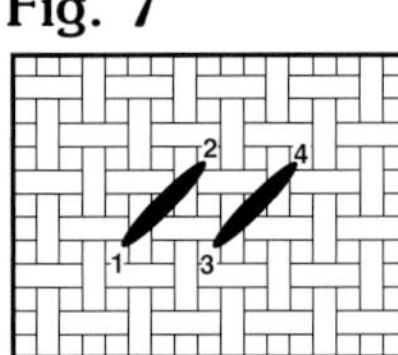

Backstitch (B'ST): For outlines and details, Backstitch should be worked after the design has been completed *(Fig. 8)*. When working over two fabric threads, work Backstitch as shown in **Fig. 9**.

Fig. 8

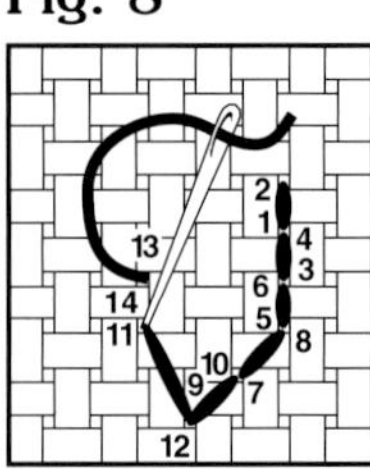

Fig. 9

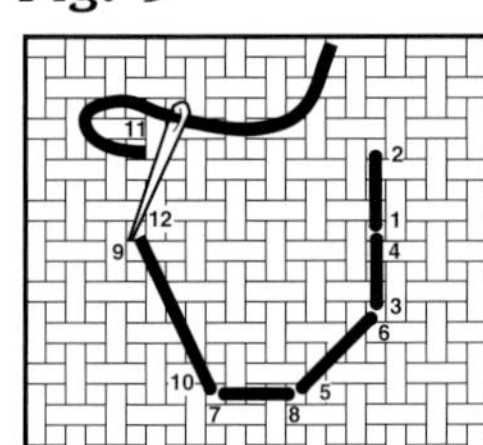

French Knot: Bring needle up at 1. Wrap floss once around needle. Insert needle at 2, tighten knot, and pull needle through fabric, holding floss until it must be released *(Fig. 10)*. For a larger knot, use more floss strands; wrap only once.

Fig. 10

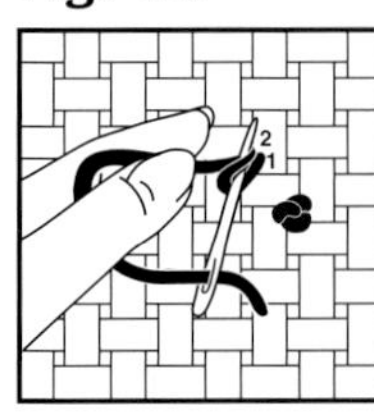

Stitching Tip

Working over Two Fabric Threads

When working over two fabric threads, the stitches should be placed so that vertical fabric threads support each stitch. Make sure that the first Cross Stitch is placed on the fabric with stitch 1-2 beginning and ending where a vertical fabric thread crosses over a horizontal fabric thread *(Fig. 11)*.

Fig. 11

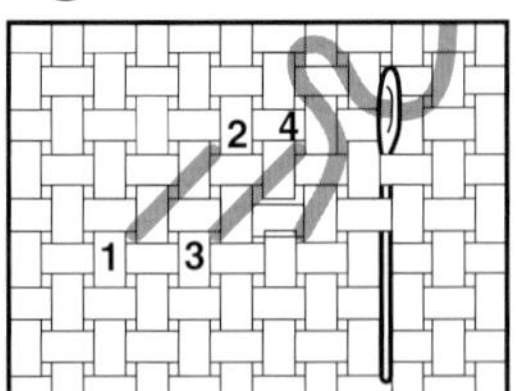